# CHOIR PRACTICE

# CHOIR PRACTICE

## THE LORE AND LURE OF POKER

## RAY P. McCORD

iUniverse, Inc.
Bloomington

# Choir Practice
# The Lore and Lure of Poker

*iUniverse books may be ordered through booksellers or by contacting:*

*iUniverse
1663 Liberty Drive
Bloomington, IN 47403
www.iuniverse.com
1-800-Authors (1-800-288-4677)*

*ISBN: 978-1-4620-5058-1 (sc)
ISBN: 978-1-4620-5059-8 (e)*

*Printed in the United States of America*

*iUniverse rev. date: 10/21/2011*

*To my uncle Harry, who had at least two women in every port, a bottle in each hand, and who introduced me to the game of poker more than seventy-five years ago. He died much too young.*

# CONTENTS

# ACKNOWLEDGEMENTS

While lazing around a pool with good food and drinks in hand originally a bunch of relatives and friends helped draft and edit the term paper from which this book has been derived. Their amateur efforts assured an A in the extension course for which the paper was written. This current effort could not have been completed without the more than able assistance and encouragement from the editors at iUniverse. And special thanks go to Martha Stewart of In House Graphics here in Salem, Oregon and to Darian Jordan, who provided the excellent illustrations.

# INTRODUCTION

This book is about the game of poker. It does not define poker terms, explain how to play, or delve into the probabilities of holding various hands or combinations thereof in a game. These things and more can be found in several of the references listed in the bibliography. It is about poker's history, heritage, and lore; and in a broad sense, it may give some idea as to why poker is played, particularly in its most popular form—hi-lo.

# I. INCEPTION

**O**nce upon a time, irregularly, not at the same place nor on the same date, but roughly at the same time on a Friday evening once each month, a select group of individuals gathered together for an activity known as "choir practice." This gathering was almost as inevitable as salmon swimming upstream to spawn or the migration of birds. The mechanism by which the members gathered was complex, consisting of repeated phone calls of entreaty, cajolery, threats, confirmation, and sometimes personal confrontation. Usually, by default, one member of the group confirmed that a quorum would be present and assured all the others that this was true. The minimum number for a quorum was six, with the magic number of seven being desirable. Rarely was the true purpose of the gathering spoken aloud. Usually the phone calls were brief and cryptic, consisting of such messages as "Choir practice … seven thirty … my house" or "My house … be there … Friday night." However, sometimes there were extended conversations about availability of regular members, possible alternates, compatibility of suggested alternates, results of the last gathering, and the possibility of procedural changes.

*Waiting for a Real Game*

Occasionally, the purpose of the gathering was referred to as a game, and the members of the group understood that the name of the game was *poker*, most often that variety known as hi-lo. With rare exception, this group met regularly and was referred to as "select" because alternates were thoroughly tested as to compatibility, playing ability, and possible conflict of interest. Those who did not qualify were not selected nor retained for participation. Being a game, and a game of cards no less, poker requires rules, regulations, and at the very least, guidelines, such as the ones illustrated in later chapters. One of the first guidelines agreed upon by the choir was that the dealer would name the game, whether it was stud, draw, or one of the many variations thereof. Another was that a joker would be included in the deck of cards to provide more variety of hands and increased probability for winners. The joker served as a fifth ace, and as a wild card in straights and flushes. Another was that the hand itself declared the winner. After much discussion, it was determined that the lowest hand was the "wheel," or ace through five, and the highest hand was the "royal flush", or ten through ace, all of one suit.

# II.   MEMBERS OF THE CHOIR

After inception, the "choir" seemed to grow just like Topsy, although some participants theorized that some esoteric form of osmosis was at work to bring a cohesive, coordinated, dedicated band into being. The original group consisted of six members: the Colonel, Dix, Three Fingers, CC, the Big Guy, and the Freeloader. Others drifted in and out to fill the seventh spot, namely two different Bobs—one a graphic artist, the other a craft work planner; Jack, Andy, Blair, and Kyle; and others who attended too infrequently to remember. If asked, the original members all claimed to be winners. Over time they probably really were winners because of their long-term relationships with one another and familiarity with one another's foibles. The infrequent attendees usually were losers just because of their infrequent attendance.

The Colonel was called this because of his long-standing intermittent efforts to qualify for a military pension. After thirty-six years, he finally achieved his goal. He became the target of choice of all the members of the group who delighted in outdoing him during practice. At one gathering where he was host, not only did they eat every crumb of his furnished snacks and drink almost all of his superb homemade apricot wine, but they also absconded with twenty-five dollars of his money. Of course, this was a low point in the Colonel's choir career.

Dix was called Dix because he just didn't like his first name, preferring his middle one, which was "Dix." When mentioned at all his first name was represented by the letter *R*. Being a real church choir member would have been entirely appropriate for him because of his ability at times to assume an innocent, angelic baby face, which usually fooled nobody in attendance. In contrast, on rare occasions, he would exhibit a fierce demeanor that sometimes was a bluff and sometimes not.

Three Fingers sometime, somewhere, lost two fingers on his right hand. This loss was never discussed by the group, nor voluntarily explained by him. It certainly did not detract from his capability to deal cards or to participate in a major role in the choir, and it lent an air of mystery to his persona. His was a steadying and calming presence, which at rare times was needed to arbitrate some dispute.

CC was the only single member of the group whose singleness did not detract from his participation. He was usually late to practice but always had some wildly amusing possibly plausible excuse. A US Navy veteran, at least once during the evening he would regale the group with some tale of past exploits while on shore leave or aboard ship. He both amazed and amused, and he never once repeated himself.

Freeloader was assigned that addition to his given name of Fred because of the Red Skelton comic character "Freddie the Freeloader." For some reason, the appellation seemed to fit. He oftentimes ambushed and surprised the other members of the choir with his ability and deceptive demeanor. Freeloader was also one of the members of the hunting group, as was the Colonel, the Big Guy, and Dix. Some of them also played golf together

The Big Guy was just that—*big*! He was not totally outsized, nor was he out of proportion. Luckily for his hunting companions he was strong enough to haul a deer out of a canyon by himself. Like so many big men he, like Three Fingers, tended to keep a calm demeanor, at least while participating in choir. He rarely missed a game, although he had a 50 mile round trip to attend.

The choir became an excellent example of the whole being much more than the sum of its oh-so-disparate parts! Each member, including alternates, had varying degrees of personal or job-related communications with the others during the workdays, belonged to one of two related organizations, and were generally considered middle class. At least five similar poker groups were identified within the organizations mentioned above, and some regular members of one group were sometimes considered as alternates for other groups. All the groups played dealer's choice, limited-bet, and mostly hi-lo poker. One group had a maximum of fifty cents bet at a time, with three raises allowed. The rest were limited to twenty-five cents, all with varied rules and procedures.

Although each group considered itself unique, this was contradicted by the fact that many millions of Americans, (to say nothing of people in other countries worldwide) are gambling billions of dollars annually at poker. It can be safely said that the game of poker appears to be so inextricably entwined with American culture that it is almost impossible to separate one from the other.

# III. LESSONS LEARNED

This time he had him! It was draw poker. He had been dealt a pair of twos and three other cards of no use, which he traded for three replacements, and he got another two and two aces in return. This time he would beat his uncle. But when he bet ten stick matches instead of the normal one or two, his uncle tossed his cards in. When asked why, his uncle explained that it was obvious because of the outsize bet that he'd been beaten. His uncle also explained that if his nephew had made a "normal" bet, he would have called or maybe raised, and his nephew would have won more matches with such a hand. His uncle also explained that even with only a pair of deuces, he could have bluffed, using the same sized bet, making his uncle think that he had a sure winning hand and causing the same result. A few hands later, the nephew decided to try the bluff, but his uncle matched his bet and won with a better hand. This time, when asked why he didn't toss in his cards, his uncle replied that he knew that his nephew was bluffing because he couldn't sit still—he was wiggling all over the place. The boy determined that he would forego bluffing and sit still, no matter what, in the future.

This whole episode took place not in a smoke-filled saloon, smoky bar, or some so-called place of ill repute, but in a smoke-filled one-room shack with a lean-to at the back. The lean-to had room for a bureau and a bed, and the shack contained a cast iron wood cook stove, a sink, a table, shelves for dishes and groceries, and a daybed. There was a window in one wall and in both doors, one in the front of the shack and one that opened to a path leading to the privy out back. At one end of the table sat a shortwave radio, emitting a feeble amount of light from its backside and spitting static and occasional faint sounds of music or a voice from its front. On opposite sides of the table sat a man and a ten year old boy with a deck of cards and an open box of farmer's matches on the table between them. One sixty-watt bulb dangled from the end of a cord hanging from the center of the ceiling, dimly illuminating the space. Cigarette butts were piled high in an ashtray at the man's elbow. The boy was growing sleepy, and his eyes burned from the cigarette smoke and staying up so late, but he did want to hear Big Ben striking the hour from London as his uncle had promised. He had gotten permission from his folks to visit his uncle just for that purpose, with the possibility of maybe even hearing Russian from Moscow, or Japanese from Tokyo, or Indonesian from Djakarta. An added benefit was that he knew that eventually he would get a foreign stamp for his collection from a postcard that confirmed that his uncle had indeed heard the radio station at a certain time and date. It was soon time, and sure enough, right on schedule, Big Ben's clanging bell could be heard by short wave from London, England, all those miles away. For whatever reason, there were no other stations to be heard that night, so the boy and his uncle decided that it was way past time for bed. And with Big Ben still resounding in his head, the boy drifted off to sleep.

The sergeant in charge came through the train car and announced that they had ten minutes to sample the coffee and doughnuts provided by the women at the station where the troop train had just stopped. There was a scramble to do just that. The poker game could wait. Shortly, all were back in their seats, with one troop sitting on a box in the aisle, with two in each seat in front of him. Someone said that they were in Utah, but he couldn't confirm it with anyone else. The group rearranged the flat piece of cardboard on their knees, one member shuffled the deck of cards, another made the cut, and the game resumed. This time it was five-card draw, and as he spread the cards in his hand, he couldn't believe what he saw. He had four aces and a queen. Naturally, he raised the first bet and everyone called. He tossed the queen, asking for one card. Two of the others argued whether he was trying to complete a straight or fill in a flush. He raised his cards in front of his face and spread them to make sure that he really had the hand that he thought he had, just as someone passing in the aisle behind him gulped and said loudly, "Oh my God." Now he knew how it felt to want to kill! And where the expression "Play 'em close to the vest" came from. In an attempt to salvage something, he bet the limit and watched as each player in turn tossed in his cards, leaving him a paltry sum instead of what should have been a real bonanza. He had had enough. He stood, gave his box seat to an eager replacement, returned to his hard passenger car seat, and sat mulling over what might have been. Over the ensuing years at other poker games he often heard the same story as having happened to someone else, one of whom was his own son.

"There I was, flat on my back, at twenty thousand feet, both engines gone." He had decided that the Air Corps mantra for any real or imagined misfortune certainly applied. Four months ago, he had arrived at his assignment, a troop carrier squadron based on Leyte in the Phillipines, and he had already flown to Milne Bay and Hollandia in New Guinea; Pelilu, Morotai, and Zamboanga on Mindanao, where "the monkeys have no tails," as one of his dad's songs went. While there, try as he might, he never did find any monkeys, let alone monkeys with no tails. There were three squadrons in the wing, all flying C-46 Curtis Commandos, which was ironic because he had sworn that he would never fly in something that couldn't shoot back. So much for that bit of bravado! Between flights, there wasn't much to do except eat, read, drink, or play cards. The problem was that when he played poker, his money disappeared so quickly that usually he had very little left at the end of two weeks into the month. Luckily, he was sending money home to be deposited in his bank account, but even so, because of his ineptness at playing high stakes poker with the senior members of the squadron, he had lost the better part of four hundred dollars in just four months. He had finally come to realize that he didn't have to play every hand to the end, and that there was absolutely no reason to try to fill any card missing inside a straight! He decided that he would continue to play only "penny ante" poker, which he did with great success, and before he came home, he won back what he had previously lost in the high stakes games. For the rest of his life, he was a winner.

# IV. POKER'S EVOLUTION

**T**homas Jefferson did not know what he had wrought. Or did he? Concerned with possible loss of the use of the Mississippi River from French control of New Orleans just after France's recovery of the Louisiana Territory from Spain Jefferson sent a delegation to Paris to negotiate the purchase of the city for the United States. Napoleon, apparently being concerned with attempting to defeat England in turn offered the whole Louisiana Territory for the sum of fifteen million dollars. This seemingly outrageous amount in reality was less than a paltry five cents an acre for a wilderness that stretched from the Mississippi River to the Rockies. In order to make the purchase money had to be borrowed from England, and on April 30, 1803 Jefferson authorized the purchase. Just as Seward's later purchase of Alaska was called Seward's Folly it would seem that Jefferson's purchase of the Louisiana territory could have been called Jefferson's folly, and possibly with better justification. However, next, Jefferson authorized the 1804-1806 Lewis and Clark Corps of Discovery trek through the wilderness and on to the Pacific and back. This whole series of events justified the United States claim to what came to be known as the Wild, Wild West, and guaranteed that the Mississippi River would remain available for use by the new American nation.

*Hand for As Nas*

Although there are no records, evidently it was sometime in the early 1800's after Jefferson's purchase that some of the French residents in New Orleans developed a game using a pack of twenty cards consisting of aces, kings, queens, jacks, and tens. This game possibly derived from a Persian game called as nas dating back several hundred years. It too consisted of a pack of twenty cards but of lions, kings, ladies, soldiers, and dancing girls dealt out to four players The limitations involved with only a twenty card deck and four players precluded any game other than showdown after betting, but did include the possibility of bluffing. There was no consideration of straights or of flushes as winning combinations.

With the Mississippi River guaranteed open to commerce the game of poker quickly spread upriver with the stern wheelers. Gradually it was adapted to the pack of fifty-two cards, which meant that more than four players could play, and increased the variety of winning combinations of cards, and of types of games. The draw appears to have been introduced during the Civil War, when soldiers on both sides spread the game's popularity. Straights and flushes arrived sometime at mid-century. and stud and jackpots came in sometime later to complete the evolution of the game to the forms known today.

*Up the Mississippi*

During this period, as poker spread upriver, and later to the West, the popular game of faro was gradually replaced in upscale saloons and especially in the low dives in the ramshackle towns along the Ohio and Mississippi River Valleys. The presence of professional gamblers on the river boats although somewhat exaggerated certainly contributed to the speedy acceptance of the game. Poker whether penny-ante or high stakes was (and is) a connoisseur's game, demanding several skills besides that of having the well-known expressionless demeanor. Other characteristics which contribute to excellence in playing the game are the ability to read body language, and some degree of acting talent. Gin poker, whiskey poker, and rum poker were variations that used lesser skills but offered the same high degree of excitement. (The bibulous names were probably applied to the variations on poker because of the sordid atmospheres in which they were played). Thus gin, whiskey, and rum poker finally became gin rummy, and 'rummy' subsequently became a family name to be applied to any of the numerous games involving the principles of melding and sequence collecting. The other general family group of games includes those in which certain cards are trumps (a corruption of the word "triumph") with which players can make "tricks." (A trick is a collective term for the cards—usually four-played and won in one round. This group includes the contract bridge and whist series of games.

# V. NAME OF THE GAME

A lthough the origins and development of the game itself seems to be well known, the origins of the name of the game are somewhat obscure. Poker could be derived from *poque*, a French card game, but poque evidently was a game of the whist family. Indeed, at one time an attempt was made to trace poker to poche, the French word for pocket Another possibility may have come from a call by non-bidding players in a German game pochspiel which call was Ich-poche. Is it even possible that poker was derived from the Hindu word pukka? Finally, another theory, and there may be more, is that, poker could originally have been underworld slang coming from the pickpocket's term for pocket book or wallet: poke so as to fool wary prey who knew the term as to what they were really after.

Besides the term "poker" itself, talk around the poker table has introduced many colorful phrases into the American language. Used in many contexts are chip in, four-flusher, high roller, I pass, joker (one not to be taken seriously), I fold, two-bit- hustler, poker face, stand

*Ray P. McCord*

pat, pass the buck, pass me, ace in the hole, call your bluff, penny ante chiseler, show down, aces, close to the vest, cold deck, and many other pokerisms ingrained into our culture and spread around the world.

# VI NOTORIETY

The first game ever reported, significantly enough, involved cheating. This was the celebrated account by an English touring actor, Joe Cowell (collected in *The Poker Game Complete*). As the very first poker kibitzer he described a game he watched aboard a steamboat going from Louisville to New Orleans in December 1829 as "a high gambling western game, founded on brag," a British game. The story referenced is one in which the professional gambler (complete with green spectacles eye shade, and diamond stickpin), evidently upset by the boat running aground, dealt the pat winning hand (four kings and one ace) to a younger player other than himself. The extent to which poker caught on in America is reflected in the pulp literature that appeared toward the end of the century. In 1896, there was even a monthly magazine called *Poker Chips*, relating little tales about poker.

From the Mississippi Valley, poker went west with the expanding frontier, and it was there that it became irrevocably entwined with the Western genre. Folk heroes like the famous gunfighter and marshal Wyatt Earp came into being. Earp's exploits as a defender of law and order have been embellished over the years with fiction, but his skill as a gambler was certainly fact. Other well-known famous or infamous, as the case may be, Westerners of the era were William Bonny, aka Billy the Kid; Buffalo Bill Cody; John Wesley Hardin; "Doc" Holiday, the consumptive dentist who backed Wyatt Earp at the famous O.K. corral shoot-out; and Pat Garret who killed Billy the Kid. Another Western gunman whose exploits have become legendary was Wild Bill Hickock. James Butler Hickock originally came west as a stagecoach driver with a reputation as a marksman. At one time or another he was in the Union Army, a scout, a gunfighter, a lawman, and a gambler. His career was enough for any two men to claim.

# VII. THE WILD, WILD WEST

The appellation Wild Bill was more than appropriate. At times he was the perfect gentleman, but at other times could become murderously violent. Illustrative of the latter is an early episode in which not being the keenest of poker players he had been regularly beaten by one sharp gambler named McDonald. Wild Bill's friends had warned him about McDonald's questionable methods of play. One night during a one-on-one high stakes game while losing badly Wild Bill had had enough. With poor judgement caused by his drinking he started to bet heavily on what seemed to be a strong hand, but McDonald matched him bet for bet. The showdown finally came and McDonald showed three jacks. Wild Bill then declared a full-house of aces and sixes and tossed his cards face down on the table. At that Mcdonald turned up Bill's cards showing only two aces and one six. Immediately, after being beaten and exposed Wild Bill whipped out a six-shooter with one hand and with the other bared his Bowie knife while at the same time declaring his pistol to be the other six and his knife to be the missing ace. 'That hand is a winner,' whispered McDonald. 'Take the pot."

Wild Bill's life alone certainly was enough to perpetuate his claim to fame (or notoriety as the case may be), but it was the circumstance of his death that made him a legend. As the story goes while riding into Deadwood, Dakota Territotory he imparted to his companions his belief that he would not leave Deadwood alive. On August 2, 1876, he was playing poker in a saloon when an acquaintance with whom he had been arguing over poker debts sneaked in and shot him in the back of the head.

*Wild Bill no Longer*

A drunken Crooked Nose McCall was the killer who took advantage of the fact that Wild Bill for once was sitting with his back exposed. He wanted to play and no one would trade for a seat against a wall. McCall was tried twice for the crime, was found guilty at the second trial, and executed.

*Dead Man's Hand*

The hand that Bill was holding almost immediately became known as a dead man's hand consisting of two pair, aces and eights, all black, and with a queen or possibly a ten as the fifth card. To this day it is rare that Bill's dead man's hand is not mentioned at least once at any given poker game. Many times this will lead to animated discussions as to the real configuration of the original hand and the possibility that in reality it was a full-house. Of course none of the participants in the discussion are experts in the subject, all have strong opinions, and the discussion almost always provides for a more than normal lively game of poker.

The violence in the west which could have been worse reminds one of the story told down through the years at poker games of the player who with no warning pinned his opponent's hand palm down to the table with his bowie knife and grated," My friend, if the ace of spades is not under your hand, I owe you an apology!'"

Another famous story concerning a showdown at gunpoint involved Le Baron Prince the then governor of the Territory of New Mexico. A native New Yorker and successful lawyer and politician he had been appointed governor by President McKinley in 1889 While watching a no-limit game in Santa Fe in 1899 he became involved in a bizarre incident with one of the south west's more notorious professional gamblers. whose remaining opponent was a well-known cattle baron from Texas. Both players got big hands, and one-hundred dollar bills were piled high on the table. With no more cash, the Texas baron wrote out the deed to his ranch and his thousands of head of cattle, tossed the paper atop the pile of money, and arrogantly challenged, "Match that if you can." The poker expert, unable to call, sent for pen and paper, wrote quickly, handed the document to the no longer governor, drew his revolver. "Sign this or I'll kill you!" he shouted. The ex-governor quickly complied. The gambler triumphantly tossed the paper into the pot. "I raise you the Territory of New Mexico! There's the deed!" The rancher swore and threw his hand in. "All right, you win," he answered, "but it's a damn good thing for you the governor of Texas isn't here!"

# IX. MUCHO MACHISMO

The previous stories are not only of the Old West but in a wild and wooly way may also exemplify the raison d'etre for poker itself. Certainly, "poker as depicted in Westerns is not really about poker at all: it is an aspect of machismo, of being a man. The game is a way of showing characters in action. The leisure time of cowboys, as it comes across in Westerns, was devoted to drinking, whoring, fighting, and playing poker, observes Philip French in his essay "Westerns" (1973). All of them are essentially male pursuits, and the only one which does not correspond to some specific physical need is poker. It seems obvious that poker is in some way central to the Western mystique. In the Wyatt Earp/ Doc Holliday films, French notes that the hero must be capable of acquitting himself well at the gaming table as proof of his manhood. At the same time, he has to keep his cool and view the game almost dispassionately; he is not really involved. Henry Fonda exemplifies this attitude in the movie, *My Darling Clementine* (1946):

"Sir, I really like poker," he declares. "Every hand has its different problems."

In fact, the poker game symbolizes, sums up in miniature, as it were, the whole Western genre. Here across the table you have the good guy and the bad guy, facing one another over the cards, the classic duel of individuals, which is what the old Western stories were all about. Indeed even with multiple players the game in reality is not about one player against a group, but one player against each other player, retaining the one on one concept.

Although subdued at today's games, machismo persists throughout Choir Practice. Particularly at the beginning of a session, it is expressed with banter about past prowess or lack thereof, with exaggeration of losses and minimization of winnings and vice-versa and predictions as to what will happen to various individuals during the game extant.

Besides the machismo involved, and poker's development paralleling that of the country, poker is without doubt the most popular international card game in history. The major reason for this worldwide popularity is due to the countless poker variations that suit temperaments of card players of all cultures. In addition, poker fits any card game situation, whether it is a serious money game among high-rolling gamblers in New York or Las Vegas, a penny ante game for the entertainment of family and friends or just for fun in the United States, Italy, England, Hong Kong, and the rest of the world over. Poker, for sure, is as characteristically American as baseball, hotdogs, and mom's apple pie. In fact, many of our more famous presidents were poker enthusiasts.

# X.  SUCCESS OR FAILURE

**❝I**n most forms of poker, the game is pure chance only until the player looks at the cards dealt him. From then on, unlike in bridge and most other card games, chance plays a lesser role, because the players need not play bad hands out to the finish. The player can throw a bad hand in and take a small loss, or perhaps, none, or he can continue to play a bad hand and sometimes win by bluffing. In rare cases a player will bluff and lose purposely in order to set up a later win. In stud and its variants, a decision can be made by the player each time another card is dealt until the showdown".

One notable game in which the original choir members participated will be left for curious amateur statisticians to calculate the odds of its occurring. The game was seven-card stud, of course, hi-lo, in which the dealer had stated that the players had to declare which way they would go—either high or low—after all bets were placed. Betting was intense, with the one obvious low hand raising each round and forcing one player with a small straight out of the game, leaving four combatants vying to take "high." The remaining four high hands unbelievably consisted of three full houses and one four of a kind. One full house dropped out before the final round of betting. Alas, the low hand not only declared "low" but also declared "high," revealing a totally concealed straight flush. Assumptions are dangerous in poker and even more so in hi-lo.

Another game played by a full slate of seven choir members was notable for its configuration and was called iron cross or sometimes crisscross. Four cards were dealt in sequence to each player, while, at the same time, five cards were dealt randomly in a cross, face down in the center of the table. The player to the dealer's left could either bet before or after one card in the perimeter was turned face up. The cards around the center card in the cross were turned in order, with the card in the center the last one to be turned. The anticipation of waiting for that last card to be turned sometimes became unbearable. One memorable turn of that center card (the joker) gave one player both the winning high (full house) and low (wheel) hands. The reader can experiment to see how this was possible, as even the players were skeptical until the cards themselves showed how it was done.

The skilled poker player will play fewer bad hands than the unskilled player, thus increasing his winning chances in a way that an equally skilled bridge player cannot do. It is at hi-lo that bluff achieves its fullest complexity, combining the concealment of five-card draw with the open card calculation of stud. As each card falls around the table at hi-lo, so the opportunities for bluff evolve, changing from card to card and player to player. The question isn't just, 'Has he got what he says he's got?' as in classical poker; it's 'Which way is he going?' and then 'Which way can I beat him?' This is the challenge of hi-lo. Bluffing does not consist of suddenly wading in with a whopping raise; it's a matter of gauging chances that are continuously changing.

Overall, one might apply to hi-lo the military or strategic concept of flexible response. Playing hi-lo requires continual responsive evaluation and reaction. Each card to each player, each bet on each round of seven-card hand, changes the situation. Assuming seven players staying to the end, which means five betting intervals one for each card turned up, and for the last down card, on which each player can bet, call, or raise, there are in theory more than one hundred decision points to be registered in a single hand. Many of these will be checks or routine calls, but each move completes the pattern. Supposing only three players see it through to the end, there will be more than fifty decision points in the hand.

# XI BLUFF OR NO

In other words, "bluff," particularly as applied in hi-lo poker, may better be termed "deception." Illustrative of both is the story heard around poker tables for many years and later made into the movie *A Big Hand for a Little Lady* (1966). As remembered the movie started with the train clanging and puffing along the station platform and gradually slowing to a stop. As usual it was late, but what was unusual was that it was only an hour late. Together a man and woman descend from the train, see that their bags are in order, converse briefly with the station master, and walk toward the bank. As in almost all western movie towns were the stable and blacksmith shop, general store, several saloons, two hotels, the bank, and a spired church at one end of the dirt street. Scattered between some of the larger buildings were private homes. Boardwalks lined the street in places with gaps where a few side streets intersected the one main street which was busy with wagons, men on horseback, pedestrians, kids, and dogs. The couple from the train caused a stir amongst the town people because the banker had let it be known that a couple was coming from St. Louis to look at some property. Obviously, these were them.

After finishing their business with the banker the couple stopped in front of the more presentable hotel while among other things she shook her finger under his nose and told him to stay away from the gambling tables. She then entered the hotel while he sauntered off down the street. Finding a saloon to his liking he entered, ordered a whiskey, and sat at a table where he was soon joined by an obvious gentleman who asked if he would be interested in a friendly game of poker. Despite his wife's admonitions in front of the whole town, and perhaps because thereof, he accepted and was introduced to four other men all of whom were town citizens. The game ran on and it was obvious that he was out of his league. He won some but lost more. He had little money left and played a final hand of five card draw.

The pot was larger than any previous one and as he picked up his cards as they were dealt he folded them together without looking at them and when he had all five in hand started to slide them apart one by one. After the third card his breath quickened, with the fourth he turned red in the face and when he saw the final card gasped and fell forward face down on the table. The only card exposed in his hand was the ace of diamonds. Pandemonium reigned. The first consensus was that his wife had to be informed. They had a dead body, but it was hers, and they had a large pot in the center of the table which at this point belonged to nobody. The arrival of the little lady quickly solved both problems. She was adamant over all male protests that she would play out her husband's hand, and told the assemblage to get the body to the undertaker. It was obvious to all that she was suffering as she dabbed daintily with her hanky at her tears and admitted that she knew very little about poker. Suddenly she exclaimed, "I know what I'll do. I'll go see the banker."

With that she exited the saloon, trudged determinedly to the bank with two of the players carefully watching the cards in her hand, and demanded to see the banker. At first he refused to listen but with the two players explaining in detail that they wanted the game to end he agreed to at least see the cards in question, he first agreed that she had the right to take her husband's place, and then perused the cards at length. Without a word he went to the safe, filled a bag with money, and motioned for her and the players out the door. At the saloon he placed the bag on the table and declared," I'm here to see that this little lady is treated fairly". The two still standing players reached for their cards on the table and threw them in the pot as one by one so did the other three players. No one got to see the hand because all had folded. The banker picked up his bag of money and left for the bank, and the lady gathered up all the money left on the table while holding her cards, stuffed everything into her handbag, demurely wiped her eyes one last time and exited the saloon.

What was the winning hand? Well, there was that ace of diamonds that everyone saw, but there was nuthin' else, partner. It was all a con-job with the banker in on it. And the last scene shows the little lady in the baggage car sitting in a comfortable chair provided by

the station master across from her husband perched on
his coffin. They have a board on their laps where after
expertly riffling the cards she deftly dealt them both a
royal flush.

# XII. THE WHANGDOODLE

Poker, of course, like all endeavors, has unwritten customs and even laws. One is that a player must know the customs or rules of the local game.

A Whangdoodle by any other name might be a Whizaroo, or a Whoopdedoo, Lolapalooza or in one case a House Special, or any other outlandish appellation fitting the environment. By whatever name this story heard down through the years is the one about the stranger who sat down to a game of poker in a cattle town. After a run of so-so hands, he picked up the ace, king, queen, jack, ten of hearts—a royal flush. Primed for the kill, he kept upping the ante until there was only one player left in the betting against him. The fellow, with the air of a man who knows he is holding the best, out of sheer compassion called his foolhardy opponent, and unveiled his dreamboat. "Royal flush," he gloated, and without bothering to look at the other's cards began raking in the pot. A brown paw reached out to detain him. "Whoa, stranger, I got a hand here that's a sight better: a Whangdoodle."

The stranger stared down in disbelief at the cards the other had laid down: a seven, five, four, trey, and a deuce—and not even in the same suit. He was reaching for his gun when one of the players caught his eye shook his head, and nodded at a sign on the wall behind the stranger. It read: "Nothing In This House Beats a Whangdoodle."

Mindful of the fact that small town poker customs vary with each community, the stranger eased his six-gun back into its holster and although unsettled continued with the game. And later, he picked up a hand containing a seven, five, four, trey, and deuce—and not in the same suit. Accordingly, he bet the limit and again found himself in a showdown with one other hand. "This time I gottcha," he announced triumphantly, "This time ain't nobody gonna beat this one." He spread his hand. "Read 'em and weep… a Whangdoodle."

The opponent, laying down a full house, shook his head commiseratingly, and pointed to another sign near the ceiling on another wall. It read: "Only One Whangdoodle a Night Per Table."

It probably is not a good idea to spring such a situation on close friends or relatives!

# XIII. LUCK O' THE INDIAN

♠ ♣ ♥ ♦

Archeological evidence shows that gambling began with the advent of civilization or perhaps sometime before, and is a human mental bias or quirk of some kind. And gambling – the struggle with fate or contest with chance is closely tied in the human mind to beliefs in the supernatural and magic.

*Lots O' Luck*

Long before the arrival of the casinos on reservations Indians were gambling. And for some of them the arrival of poker with the white man's invasion of the west was an enhancement of already established behaviors. One chief of one tribe, both of which shall remain nameless, was one of those who in today's world would be identified as addicted to gambling. As a chief he arrogantly expected that he should win every time at poker which of course by its very nature he didn't. Frustrated that he could not win in every game he played he consulted with the senior shaman well known for the accuracy of his predictions and advice. He explained that he wanted some how to confidently play every game of poker knowing that he would win. The shaman wisely advised that if he won every time that he would soon have no one to play with. Grudgingly the chief acknowledged that to be true, but insisted that he wanted some sort of advantage. The shaman finally agreed to direct him on the proper steps to obtaining what he wanted.

"First of all", he said, "You must go to the Great South Butte, climb to the top, fast with no water, and while watching the sunrise, pray to the packrats to grant your wish for power at poker". The chief scoffed at this, but finally did as he was told. He returned to the shaman and accused him of fraud, but the shaman very calmly said, "I didn't say it would be easy, here is what you must do now. Go to the place that looks like the moon, but this time pray each day for two days to the packrats at sunrise for what you want, and return here. This time the chief was furious, and after venting his rage on a few innocent rocks and trees while on his way back to the shaman became unnaturally calm by the time he arrived. The shaman praised him for his tenacity, and told him, "This now is the final step, and here is what you must do. You must trek for seven days to the land of many smokes where you will fast with no water, chew the buttons I give you, and perform as before for three days." He did as told and at the third sunrise the grandfather of all packrats appeared and promised to fulfill the chief's wishes.

*Grandfather Packrat*

The grandfather packrat told the chief to scrape the residue formed by his pee on the ground, place it in a buckskin bag, and carry it around his neck. He taught the chief three songs to sing before playing poker, and instructed him to wash all decorations thoroughly from his body with wood ash before a game. "If you do so you will almost always win", he stated. The chief had great success until in his eagerness after a war dance to get to a game he neglected to sing and wash. The effects nearly killed him, he never played again, and every day sat on the porch of the trading post where he was called chief mumbles until he died.

# XIV. MAXIMIZING THE ODDS

The Indians are not alone in their beliefs, not by a long shot. What about the lucky seat, or the rituals players so often perform in the way they get settled down. Some like a special position at the table or even a particular chair, or wear something special, or stack their chips or money in a certain way. Once in a while a player will parade around the table at least three times before choosing a seat. All of these are compulsive little habits which are supposed to induce success. One choir member drives all over town to find green traffic lights when coming to a game, so that he can get the feeling of everything going right for him.

Gamblers, as a class, are perhaps the most fervent believers in lucky charms and conversely in unlucky omens. To pass another person on a staircase on the way to a gaming room is to be avoided like the plague, as it is believed to signify a cross, which offends the "Moody Goddess of Chance" and causes her to negate your luck for the upcoming game.

When cutting cards, you must never cut crosswise if

you wish to win, and you should leave a game as quickly as you can after dropping (or flicking out) a card from the pack because this is a sign that 'Lady Luck' is about to move elsewhere. Even worse is dropping a card on the floor. Frequently you will find players changing their seats or calling for a new pack of cards in the belief that the change will extend their luck. You may also change your luck by walking around your seat from left to right, which will invalidate the bad luck by enclosing it in a circle. Another method of changing your luck is to slip a handkerchief under yourself, thereby changing your base, or sit on one hand for a while, thus making a new start. Gamblers will carry an infinite number of lucky charms on themselves, anything from a rabbit's foot to a rusty horseshoe nail. Amulets made from an endless variety of materials such as precious stones, worthless stones picked from a beach, scarabs, special coins pixies, children's teeth, elephant's hair, you name it, and no matter how bizarre, some superstitious gambler somewhere has got it in his (or her) pocket.

The hope of gain with the fear of loss is the catalyst that creates a highly charged atmosphere in most gaming rooms. In this emotional climate, as a player you are generally exposed to forces that are stronger than the rational thinking of your ordinary workaday world, which sends you back to your ancestral belief in magic. "Beginner's luck", for example, is based on the Stone Age superstitious belief in the "magic" of new things.

There are many rules you must follow if you wish to stay on good terms with the "Goddess of Chance". You must never indicate that she is on your side, for this constitutes "bragging" and is a temptation for fate to intervene. You must never sing nor whistle while gambling because using the vocal chords disperses your power while silence conserves it. You must always avoid transferring your luck to others, and so you must not, if you wish to avoid disaster, lend money to another gambler, as this symbolizes disposing of some of your luck by transmitting it to someone else.

And when you blow on the cards or dice aren't you trying, essentially, to blow the breath of life back into a failing corporeality?

# XV. FINALE

So this is poker—its lure and lore, its history, heritage, machismo, superstition, and magic. And when all is said and done if indeed you must play the game; then learn how to hold 'em, learn when to fold 'em, when to walk away, and, particularly when to run. And run *FAST!*

One final word from the losers: *DEAL!*

# *BIBLIOGRAPHY

1. John K. Hutchens, *The Gambler's Bedside Book* (Taplinger Publishing Co., Inc., 1977)1.

2. Oswald Jacoby, *Penny Ante and Up* (Doubleday & Company, Inc., 1979).

3. .Irv Roddy, *Friday Night Poker or Penny Poker for Million,s* Simon & Schuster, 1961).

4. Edwin Silberstang *Winning Poker Strategy,* (David McKay Company, Inc., 1930).

5. John Scarne, *Scarne's Guide to Modern Poker* (Simon & Schuster, A Division of Gulf & Western Corporation, 1979),

6. David Spanier, *Total Poker* (Simon and Schuster, A Gulf &Western Company)

*Ray P. McCord*

7. Taetzch, *Winning Methods of Bluffing and Betting in Poker* (Drake Publishers Inc., 1976)

8. Alan Wykes, *The Complete Illustrated Guide to Gambling* (Doubleday & Company Inc., 1964),

9. Norman Zadeh, *Winning Poker Systems* (Prentice-Hall, Inc., 1974).

# AFTERWORD

nyone who has read to this point in the book has noticed the lack of any reference to the Texas Hold Em phenomenon. This is because the members of the choir had not heard of Texas Hold Em until after they had been practicing for quite a while. For some reason the game did not appeal to the members of the choir and after being discovered was played only once or twice per session. More information about the game than anyone should rightly expect can be found on line at Google.

Choir Practice includes a bibliography from which works many direct and extensive quotes were used in the original manuscript written as a term paper for an Idaho State extension anthropology class some 30 years ago. Permission to use the same quotes was requested of publishers as required with not one response. Therefore all the direct quotes were altered and/or rewritten as original by the writer.

The illustration on page 55 is the collective impression of the Colonel by the other members of the choir after his last session before leaving for greener pastures in a land far, far away. Much to their chagrin it was less than three years before he returned to again challenge their prowess in the field of poker.

BOB JOHNSTON
-1974-